THE 100
FUNNIEST
KIDS JOKES
OF ALL TIME

The 100 Funniest Kids Jokes of All Time
Copyright © 2020 Victor Junior
www.victor-junior.com

All rights reserved. This book or any portion thereof may not be reproduced or used in any manner whatsoever without the express written permission of the publisher.

1st Edition, 2020
Innovate Publishing
www.innovatepublishing.ca

ISBN (Paperback): 978-1-7774451-7-1

This book belongs to

What does lightning wear under its pants?

Thunderwear!

Why do ducks have feathers on their tails?

To cover their buttquacks.

Why was the sand wet?

Because the sea weed.

What kind of music do mummies listen to?

Wrap music.

What do
sea monsters
eat for lunch?

Fish and ships

What do you get when you cross a snowman and a vampire?

Frostbite!

What's an astronaut's favourite part of a computer?

The space bar

How does a penguin build a house?

Igloos it together

Where do you learn all about ice cream?

Sundae school

Why don't koalas have jobs?

Because they don't have the koala-fications

Why do you never let a bear hold the remote?

Because he'll keep pressing the paws button

I was wondering why the frisbee kept looking bigger and bigger and bigger.

Then it hit me.

How does Darth Vader like his toast?

On the dark side

What do you call a dinosaur fart?

A blast from the past

Why don't eggs tell jokes?

Because they'd crack each other up

What do cows watch on Netflix?

Moo-vies

Why do you have to watch out for ninja farts?

Because they're silent, but deadly

Why did the dinosaur cross the road?

Because chickens weren't invented yet

Why don't skeletons fart in public?

Because they don't have the guts

Why did the M&M go to school?

Because he wanted to be a Smartie

Why is farting in an elevator bad?

Because it smells on so many levels

What do you call a blind dinosaur?

Do-you-think-
-he-saurus

Why do Piglet and Tigger smell?

Because they're always playing with Pooh

Why don't people like clown farts?

Because they smell funny

Why did the *God of Thunder* need to stretch his muscles when he was a kid?

Because he was a little Thor

How can you tell if a vampire is sick?

Because he's always coffin

Why should you never fart in the Apple store?

Because they don't have Windows

Where do cows go on December 31?

A Moo Year's Eve party

What's blue and smells like red paint?

Blue paint

Why should you never tell a pig a secret?

Because they always squeal

How do elves learn how to spell?

They learn the elf-abet

What's invisible and smells like carrots?

A rabbit's fart

What do you call a bear with no teeth?

A gummy bear

Why can't you hear a pterodactyl use the toilet?

Because the "p" is silent

Why can't you give Elsa a balloon?

Because she'll *Let It Go*

What did Obi-Wan say to Luke Skywalker when he couldn't use chopsticks?

"Use the forks, Luke"

What do you call cheese that isn't yours?

Nacho cheese!

Where do sheep go to get haircuts?

The baa-baa shop

Where do rabbits go after they get married?

On a bunny-moon

Why is Cinderella bad at soccer?

Because she's always running away from the ball

What does Aquaman say to his kids when they won't eat dinner?

Water you waiting for?

What is the strongest animal in the ocean?

Mussels

Why do you never see elephants hiding in trees?

Because they're so good at it

How did the barber win the race?

Because he knew a short cut

What don't sharks eat clownfish?

Because they taste funny

Why don't lobsters share their fries?

Because they're shell-fish

Why are basketball courts always wet?

Because the players are always dribbling

Why should you never trust stairs?

Because they're always up to something

What kind of dog does Dracula have?

A bloodhound

Who gives sharks presents at Christmas?

Santa Jaws

Who gives dogs presents at Christmas?

Santa Paws

What do you call a famous turtle?

A shell-ebrity

How do oceans say hello to each other?

They wave!

What's a pirate's favourite letter?

Rrrrrrr!

What did
0 say to 8?

"Nice belt!"

Why do bees have sticky hair?

Because they use honey combs

What do hedgehogs say when they hug?

"Ouch!"

What kind of shoes do ninjas wear?

Sneakers

Why is a bad joke like a broken pencil?

Because it has no point

What did the banana say to the apple?

Nothing.
Fruit can't talk!

What has four wheels and flies?

A garbage truck

What kind of key can never unlock a door?

A monkey

What do you call a bear with no ears?

A "b"

What goes black-white-black-white-black-white?

A penguin falling down a hill

What's black & white and says "Hahaha"?

The penguin that pushed him

Why did Mickey Mouse go into space?

He was looking for Pluto

Why was the clock sent to the principal's office?

Because he was tocking too much

Why was 6 afraid of 7?

Because 7, 8, 9

Which food is never on time?

Choco-late

What did one volcano say to the other?

"I lava you!"

What is the smartest insect?

A spelling bee

Which superhero always hits a home run?

Batman

Why is a hockey stadium always cold?

Because it has lots of fans

What kind of math do birds love?

Owl-gebra

Why did the banana go to the doctor?

Because he wasn't peeling well

What is a cat's favourite colour?

Purrrr-ple

Why was the rabbit upset?

Because he was having a bad hare day

Which nut has the most money?

A cashew

How do you throw a party in space?

You have to planet

What kind of photos do turtles take?

Shell-fies

What is Spiderman's favorite month?

Web-uary

What goes up but never comes down?

Your age

What kind of haircuts do bees get?

Buzzzzcuts

What starts with
the letter T,
ends with the letter T
and has T in it?

A teapot

What do you call a witch who lives in the desert?

A sand-wich

What happened to the boy who only ate Skittles?

He farted rainbows

How do you fix a broken jack-o-lantern?

With a pumpkin patch

Why did the dad stop telling fart jokes?

Because everyone told him they stink

Poo jokes are not my favourite.

But they're a solid number two

Which monster is always playing tricks?

Prank-enstein

What did the poo say to the fart?

You blow me away

Why did the football coach go to the bank?

To get his quarterback

What do you get when you cross a cow and a trampoline?

A milkshake

What do you call an elephant at the North Pole?

Lost

Why is Peter Pan always flying?

Because he Neverlands

Why was the broom late for school?

Because it over swept

What do you call a train carrying bubble-gum?

A chew-chew train

If you have 9 apples in one hand and 7 oranges in your other hand, what do you have?

REALLY big hands

Why are Superman's costumes so tight?

Because they're all Size "S"

What do you call a droid that takes the long way around?

R2-Detour

What do you call a pig with a black belt in karate?

A Pork CHOP!

FROM THE AUTHOR

Thanks for reading *The 100 Funniest Kids Jokes of All Time*.

I really hope you, your friends, and your family enjoyed it!

As a small business and self-employed writer, my Amazon review rating means everything for my success and continued growth.

If you can spare a few moments to leave a positive Amazon review it would go a long way towards helping others decide about my books.

Thank you and I look forward to seeing you again in the next book!

CHECK OUT OUR OTHER TITLES:

THE 100 GREATEST KIDS RIDDLES OF ALL TIME

THE 100 GREATEST KNOCK KNOCK JOKES OF ALL TIME

THE 100 GREATEST DAD JOKES OF ALL TIME

THE 100 GREATEST PARENTING JOKES OF ALL TIME

100 *MORE* OF THE GREATEST DAD JOKES OF ALL TIME

Manufactured by Amazon.ca
Bolton, ON